Multiplication
MELTDOWN

Lisa Arias

Rourke
Educational Media

rourkeeducationalmedia.com

Scan for Related Titles
and Teacher Resources

Before Reading:

Building Academic Vocabulary and Background Knowledge

Before reading a book, it is important to tap into what your child or students already know about the topic. This will help them develop their vocabulary, increase their reading comprehension, and make connections across the curriculum.

1. *Look at the cover of the book. What will this book be about?*
2. *What do you already know about the topic?*
3. *Let's study the Table of Contents. What will you learn about in the book's chapters?*
4. *What would you like to learn about this topic? Do you think you might learn about it from this book? Why or why not?*
5. *Use a reading journal to write about your knowledge of this topic. Record what you already know about the topic and what you hope to learn about the topic.*
6. *Read the book.*
7. *In your reading journal, record what you learned about the topic and your response to the book.*
8. *After reading the book complete the activities below.*

Content Area Vocabulary
Read the list. What do these words mean?

common factor

composite numbers

denominator

factor rainbows

factors

fraction

greatest common factor

least common multiple

multiples

numerator

prime

prime factorization

simplify

After Reading:

Comprehension and Extension Activity

After reading the book, work on the following questions with your child or students in order to check their level of reading comprehension and content mastery.

1. *Why are images such as rainbows and cakes used to explain math concepts? (Asking questions)*
2. *Explain how factor rainbows work. (Summarize)*
3. *Why is finding the least common denominator of two fractions helpful? (Infer)*
4. *What are factors? (Summarize)*
5. *How are factor rainbows and finding the greatest common factor of two numbers related? (Asking questions)*

Extension Activity

Let's create a factor tree! Visuals such as a rainbow and a cake are helpful while learning math concepts. Now let's put your knowledge to the test by creating a factor tree. Using a piece of paper and marker, draw a tree trunk in the middle of the page. Write any number on the tree trunk to factor. Now, draw the roots of the tree with all the possible factors. Finish your math factor tree by drawing branches and leaves. How does this factor tree visual help you learn factors? What do the factors represent on the tree?

Table of Contents

Factors

Have no doubt, you will soon learn what **factors** and **multiples** are all about.

Factors are how we will start.

No need to explore
because you have seen them before.

In multiplication, factors are the numbers being multiplied.

$$6 \times 4 = 24$$

Factors

Multiplication Chart

1 × 1 = 1	2 × 1 = 2	3 × 1 = 3	4 × 1 = 4
1 × 2 = 2	2 × 2 = 4	3 × 2 = 6	4 × 2 = 8
1 × 3 = 3	2 × 3 = 6	3 × 3 = 9	4 × 3 = 12
1 × 4 = 4	2 × 4 = 8	3 × 4 = 12	4 × 4 = 16
1 × 5 = 5	2 × 5 = 10	3 × 5 = 15	4 × 5 = 20
1 × 6 = 6	2 × 6 = 12	3 × 6 = 18	4 × 6 = 24
1 × 7 = 7	2 × 7 = 14	3 × 7 = 21	4 × 7 = 28
1 × 8 = 8	2 × 8 = 16	3 × 8 = 24	4 × 8 = 32
1 × 9 = 9	2 × 9 = 18	3 × 9 = 27	4 × 9 = 36
1 × 10 = 10	2 × 10 = 20	3 × 10 = 30	4 × 10 = 40
1 × 11 = 11	2 × 11 = 22	3 × 11 = 33	4 × 11 = 44
1 × 12 = 12	2 × 12 = 24	3 × 12 = 36	4 × 12 = 48

5 × 1 = 5	6 × 1 = 6	7 × 1 = 7	8 × 1 = 8
5 × 2 = 10	6 × 2 = 12	7 × 2 = 14	8 × 2 = 16
5 × 3 = 15	6 × 3 = 18	7 × 3 = 21	8 × 3 = 24
5 × 4 = 20	6 × 4 = 24	7 × 4 = 28	8 × 4 = 32
5 × 5 = 25	6 × 5 = 30	7 × 5 = 35	8 × 5 = 40
5 × 6 = 30	6 × 6 = 36	7 × 6 = 42	8 × 6 = 48
5 × 7 = 35	6 × 7 = 42	7 × 7 = 49	8 × 7 = 56
5 × 8 = 40	6 × 8 = 48	7 × 8 = 56	8 × 8 = 64
5 × 9 = 45	6 × 9 = 54	7 × 9 = 63	8 × 9 = 72
5 × 10 = 50	6 × 10 = 60	7 × 10 = 70	8 × 10 = 80
5 × 11 = 55	6 × 11 = 66	7 × 11 = 77	8 × 11 = 88
5 × 12 = 60	6 × 12 = 72	7 × 12 = 84	8 × 12 = 96

9 × 1 = 9	10 × 1 = 10	11 × 1 = 11	12 × 1 = 12
9 × 2 = 18	10 × 2 = 20	11 × 2 = 22	12 × 2 = 24
9 × 3 = 27	10 × 3 = 30	11 × 3 = 33	12 × 3 = 36
9 × 4 = 36	10 × 4 = 40	11 × 4 = 44	12 × 4 = 48
9 × 5 = 45	10 × 5 = 50	11 × 5 = 55	12 × 5 = 60
9 × 6 = 54	10 × 6 = 60	11 × 6 = 66	12 × 6 = 72
9 × 7 = 63	10 × 7 = 70	11 × 7 = 77	12 × 7 = 84
9 × 8 = 72	10 × 8 = 80	11 × 8 = 88	12 × 8 = 96
9 × 9 = 81	10 × 9 = 90	11 × 9 = 99	12 × 9 = 108
9 × 10 = 90	10 × 10 = 100	11 × 10 = 110	12 × 10 = 120
9 × 11 = 99	10 × 11 = 110	11 × 11 = 121	12 × 11 = 132
9 × 12 = 108	10 × 12 = 120	11 × 12 = 132	12 × 12 = 144

This chart is so clever,
with all the factors listed together.

Factor Rainbows

Time to take some numbers apart.
Factoring is exactly where we will start.

Finding factors using **factor rainbows** is fun to do.
Just begin with the factor of 1 and then try 2.

Continue in order until you reach a factor already used.

Once complete, make a list of the factors... nice and neat.

Factor Rainbow for **24**

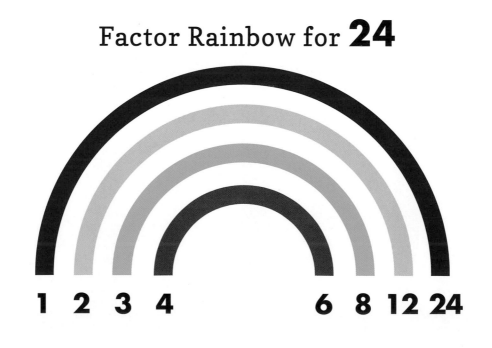

1 2 3 4   6 8 12 24

Factor Rainbow for **12**

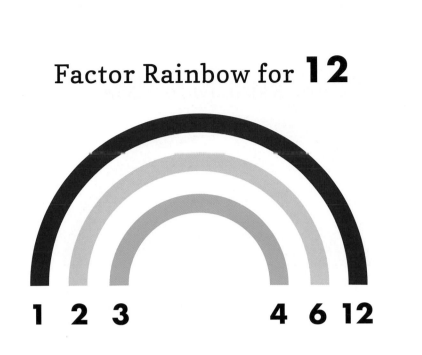

1 2 3   4 6 12

Factor Rainbow for **25**

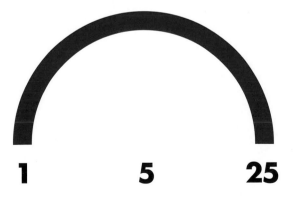

1   5   25

When a factor can be multiplied by itself, put that factor in the middle of your rainbow.

Practice makes perfect. Let's try some more.
Soon you'll know factors galore.

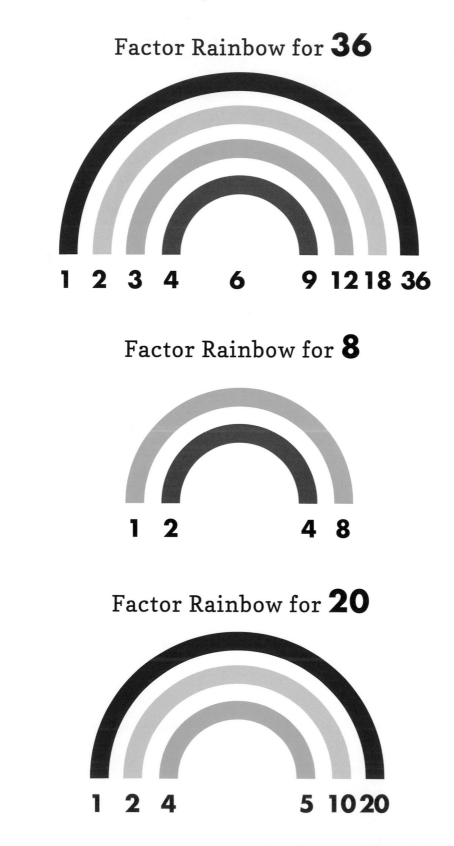

Factor Rainbow for **36**

1 2 3 4 6 9 12 18 36

Factor Rainbow for **8**

1 2 4 8

Factor Rainbow for **20**

1 2 4 5 10 20

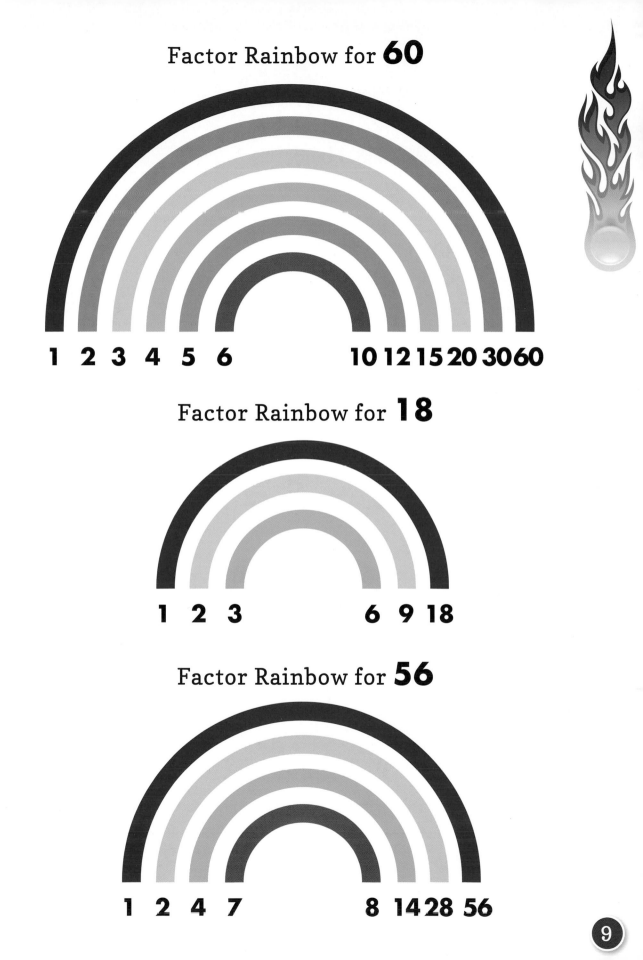

Factor Rainbow for **60**

1 2 3 4 5 6   10 12 15 20 30 60

Factor Rainbow for **18**

1 2 3   6 9 18

Factor Rainbow for **56**

1 2 4 7   8 14 28 56

Prime Numbers

Sometimes you can run into a bind,
when your rainbow only has one line.

When the only factors of a number
are one and itself, it is a **prime** number.

When this happens, your rainbow is small,
without very much color at all.

$$1 \times 5 = 5$$

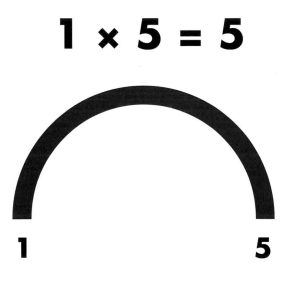

1   5

You can easily see 5 is prime.
The only factors of 5 are 1 and 5.

Prime and Composite Numbers

Take a moment to find the prime numbers to 100.

There is no pattern to use, just the factor of 1 to choose.

1	**2**	**3**	4	**5**	6	**7**	8	9	10
11	12	**13**	14	15	16	**17**	18	**19**	20
21	22	**23**	24	25	26	27	28	**29**	30
31	32	33	34	35	36	**37**	38	39	40
41	42	**43**	44	45	46	**47**	48	49	50
51	52	**53**	54	55	56	57	58	**59**	60
61	62	63	64	65	66	**67**	68	69	70
71	72	**73**	74	75	76	77	78	**79**	80
81	82	**83**	84	85	86	87	88	**89**	90
91	92	93	94	95	96	**97**	98	99	100

The other numbers on the chart are called composites.

Composite numbers have factors other than 1, allowing you to have some factor fun.

The numbers 0 and 1 are not considered prime or composite.

Prime, Composite, or Neither

Have you got all that? It's not time for a breather.
Decide, are these numbers prime, composite, or neither?

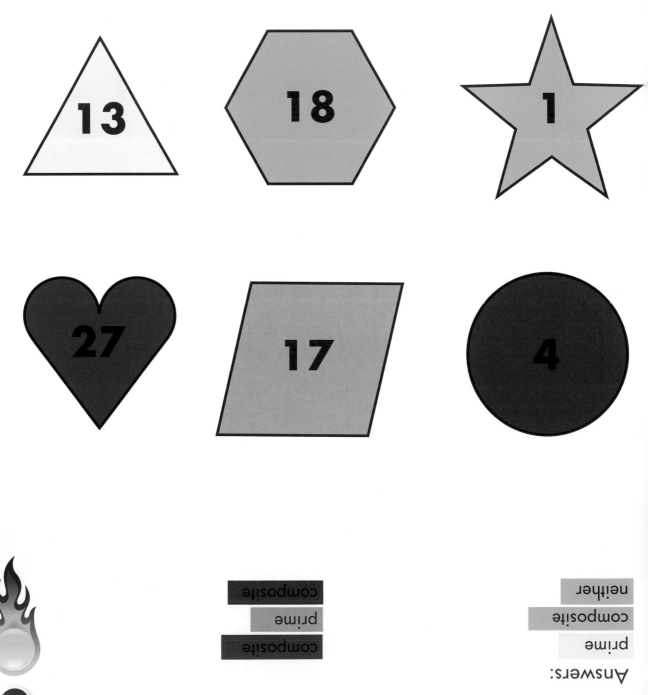

Answers:
prime
composite
neither

composite
prime
composite

Common Factors

Sometimes you will be asked to share the common factors of a number pair.

To do so, take each number from the pair and list the factors that they share.

The factors for **18** are ①, **2,** ③, **6,** ⑨, **18**

The factors for **27** are ①, ③, ⑨, **27**

The common factors of **18** and **27** are ①, ③, and ⑨

Greatest Common Factor

The **greatest common factor** is the largest factor that two or more numbers share.

List the factors of each number, no matter how small and pick the largest **common factor** of them all.

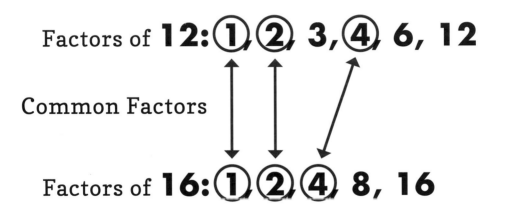

Factors of **12:** ①, ②, 3, ④, 6, 12

Common Factors

Factors of **16:** ①, ②, ④, 8, 16

4 is the greatest common factor.

You can use GCF as a shortcut for greatest common factor.

Find the greatest common factor of each set of numbers.

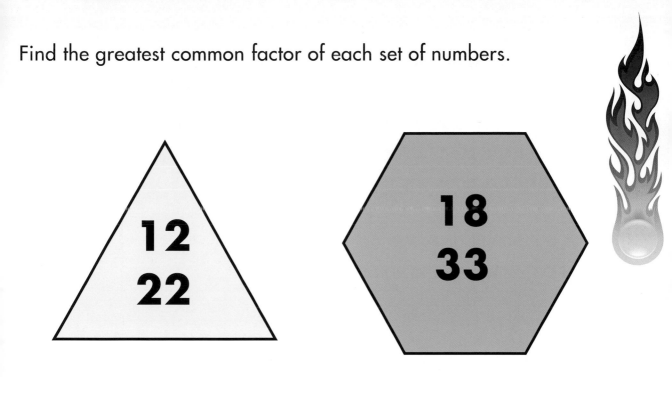

12
22

18
33

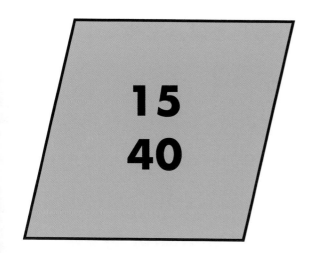

15
40

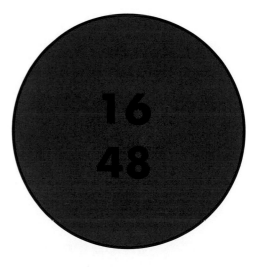

16
48

Time to Simplify!

The greatest common factor is a fabulous tool
to **simplify** fractions when you're in school.

It takes a moment or two to do,
but will be very useful to you.

$$\frac{24}{32}$$ ⟵● Numerator

⟵● Denominator

24: 1, 2, 3, 4, 6, ⑧, 12, 24
32: 1, 2, 4, ⑧, 16, 32

8 is the greatest common factor.

To simplify, divide the **numerator** and **denominator** by the greatest common factor.

$$\frac{24}{32} \div \frac{8}{8} = \frac{3}{4}$$

16

Divide by the greatest common factor to simplify each **fraction**.

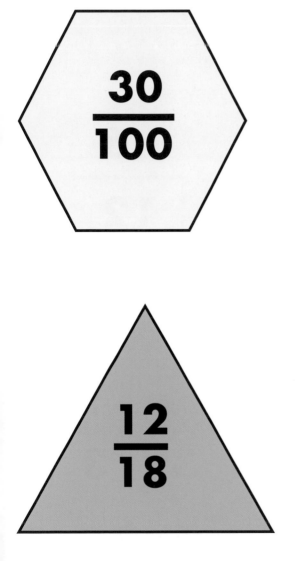

$$\frac{30}{100}$$

$$\frac{8}{10}$$

$$\frac{12}{18}$$

$$\frac{5}{25}$$

Prime Factorization

Factoring a number is fun to do,
but finding its **prime factorization** is very cool.

It is time to celebrate by making a birthday cake!

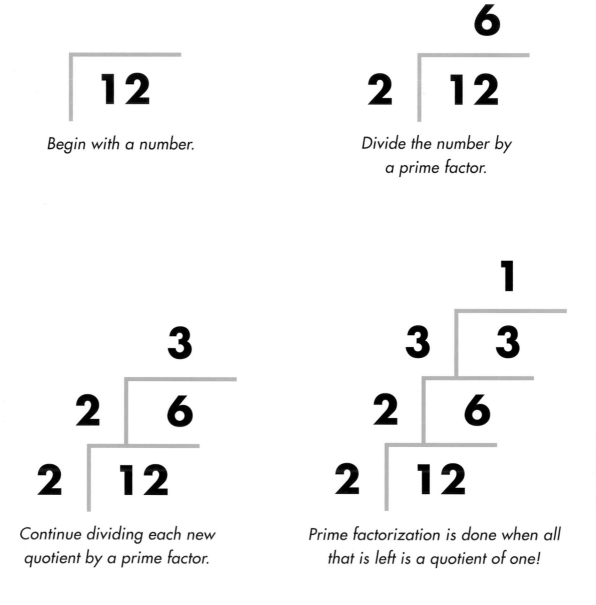

Begin with a number.

Divide the number by
a prime factor.

Continue dividing each new
quotient by a prime factor.

Prime factorization is done when all
that is left is a quotient of one!

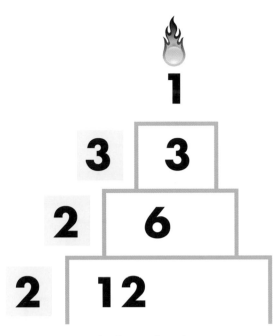

1

3 | **3**

2 | **6**

2 | **12**

Finish the cake shape.

The prime factorization of **12** is

2 × **2** × **3**

It's not yet time to take a break,
let's practice making some more cake!

Find the prime factorization of each number.

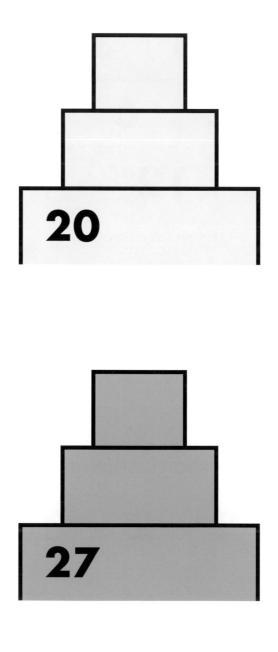

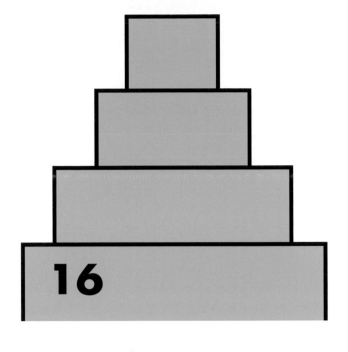

16

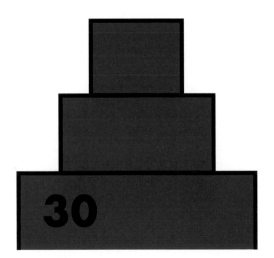

30

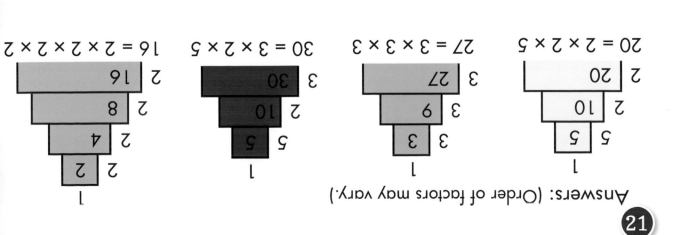

Multiples

Now our factoring fun is done. Let's take some time to learn how loveable multiples can be.

Multiples are easy to find.
If you take a number and skip count it you'll be just fine.

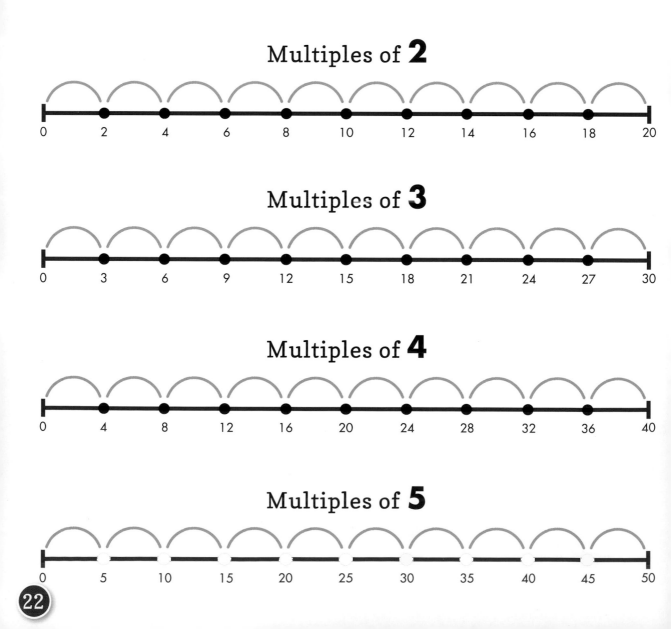

Multiples of **2**

| 0 | 2 | 4 | 6 | 8 | 10 | 12 | 14 | 16 | 18 | 20 |

Multiples of **3**

| 0 | 3 | 6 | 9 | 12 | 15 | 18 | 21 | 24 | 27 | 30 |

Multiples of **4**

| 0 | 4 | 8 | 12 | 16 | 20 | 24 | 28 | 32 | 36 | 40 |

Multiples of **5**

| 0 | 5 | 10 | 15 | 20 | 25 | 30 | 35 | 40 | 45 | 50 |

Multiples of **6**

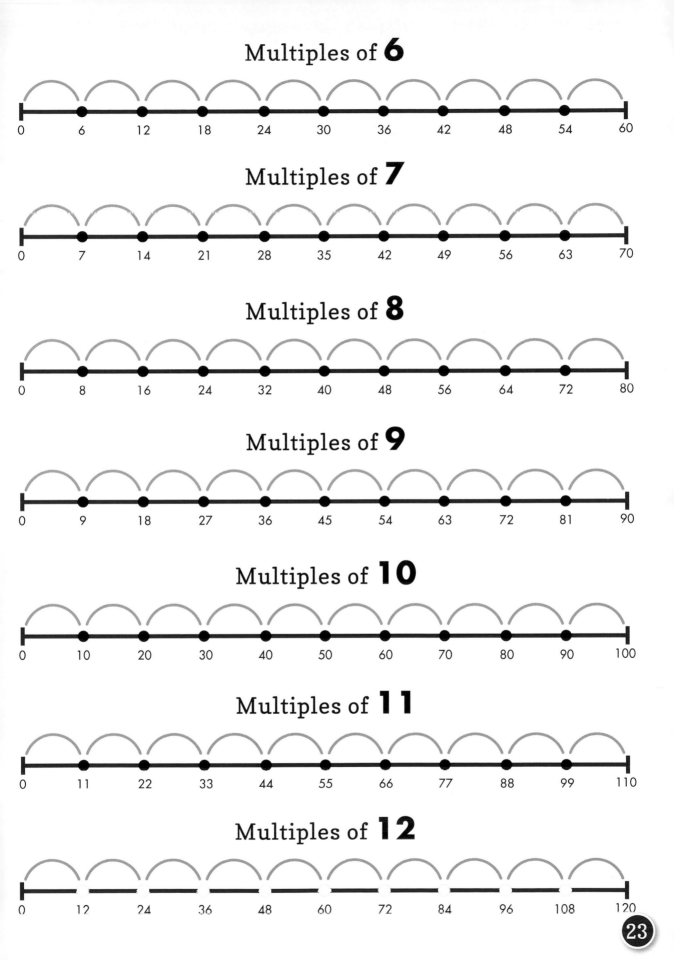

| 0 | 6 | 12 | 18 | 24 | 30 | 36 | 42 | 48 | 54 | 60 |

Multiples of **7**

| 0 | 7 | 14 | 21 | 28 | 35 | 42 | 49 | 56 | 63 | 70 |

Multiples of **8**

| 0 | 8 | 16 | 24 | 32 | 40 | 48 | 56 | 64 | 72 | 80 |

Multiples of **9**

| 0 | 9 | 18 | 27 | 36 | 45 | 54 | 63 | 72 | 81 | 90 |

Multiples of **10**

| 0 | 10 | 20 | 30 | 40 | 50 | 60 | 70 | 80 | 90 | 100 |

Multiples of **11**

| 0 | 11 | 22 | 33 | 44 | 55 | 66 | 77 | 88 | 99 | 110 |

Multiples of **12**

| 0 | 12 | 24 | 36 | 48 | 60 | 72 | 84 | 96 | 108 | 120 |

Common Multiples

Sometime you may be asked to share
the common multiples of a number pair.

Take each number from the pair
and list the multiples that they share.

Multiples of **3:**

3, 6, 9, (12), 15, 18, 21, (24)...

Multiples of **4:**

4, 8, (12), 16, 20, (24), 28...

From the list of the factors you see, find a common factor for you and me.

Multiples of **3:**

3, 6, 9, 12, 15, 18, 21, 24

Multiples of **4:**

4, 8, 12, 16, 20, 24, 28, 32

Multiples of **6:**

6, 12, 18, 24, 30, 36, 42, 48

Multiples of **8:**

8, 16, 24, 32, 40, 48, 56, 64

Least Common Multiple

To find the **least common multiple** of numbers, list the multiples for each and pick the smallest (least) multiple that the numbers have in common.

Finding the least common multiple is so simple.
Let's take a look at the example.

6: 6, 12, ⑱, 24, 30...
9: 9, ⑱, 27, 36, 45...

The least common multiple of **6** and **9** is **18**.

You can use LCM as a shortcut for least common multiple.

The least common multiple of 3 and 4 is 12. Why?

Multiples of **3**:
3, 6, 9, (12), 15, 18, 21, 24

Multiples of **4**:
4, 8, (12), 16, 20, 24

Least Common Denominator

When the need for common denominators appear,
the least common multiple better be near.

The least common denominator is the least common multiple of the denominators.

Find the least common denominator of $\dfrac{1}{8}$ and $\dfrac{5}{12}$

To find the least common denominator of a **fraction** pair, list the multiples of the denominators, fair and square.

8: 8, 16, ⃝24, 32, 40, 48

12: 12, ⃝24, 36, 48

24 is the least common denominator of $\dfrac{1}{8}$ and $\dfrac{5}{12}$

Find the least common denominator of these fractions.

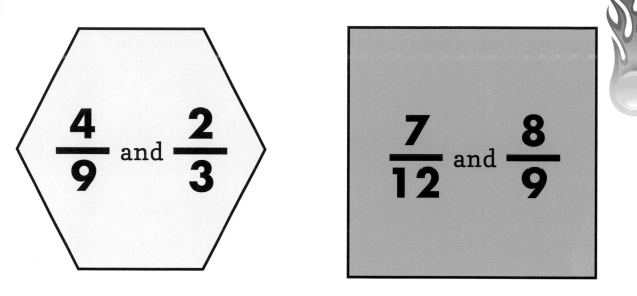

$$\frac{4}{9} \text{ and } \frac{2}{3}$$

$$\frac{7}{12} \text{ and } \frac{8}{9}$$

$$\frac{11}{12} \text{ and } \frac{7}{8}$$

Glossary

common factor (KOM-uhn FAK-tur): a number that is a factor of two or more numbers

composite numbers (kuhm-POZ-it NUHM-burz): numbers with factors other than zero and one

denominator (di-NOM-uh-nay-tur): the bottom number in a fraction that tells how many equal parts there are

factor rainbows (FAK-tur RAYN-bohs): charts used to show factors of a number

factors (FAK-turz): the numbers that are multiplied

fraction (FRAK-shuhn): a number that is part of a group or part of a whole

greatest common factor (GRAYT-est KOM-uhn FAK-tur): the largest number that is a common factor of two or more numbers

least common multiple (LEEST KOM-uhn MUHL-tuh-puhl): the smallest multiple that two or more numbers share

multiples (MUHL-tuh-puhls): the product of two counting numbers

numerator (NOO-muh-ray-tur): the top number in a fraction that tells how many parts of the denominator are taken

prime (PRIME): a number with only two factors, one and itself

prime factorization (PRIME FAK-tur-uh-za-shuhn): finding the prime factors of a number

simplify (SIM-pluh-fye): to reduce a fraction to its lowest terms

Index

Websites to Visit

www.fun4thebrain.com/beyondfacts/lcmsnowball.html

www.quia.com/cb/8436.html

jmathpage.com/JIMSMultiplicationfactorsandmultiples.html

About the Author

Lisa Arias is a math teacher who lives in Tampa, Florida with her husband and two children. Her out-of-the-box thinking and love for math guided her toward becoming an author. She enjoys playing board games and spending time with family and friends.

Meet The Author!
www.meetREMauthors.com

PHOTO CREDITS: Cover: © Misha, sommerby; Page 3: © CTRd

Edited by: Jill Sherman

Cover and Interior design by: Tara Raymo

Library of Congress PCN Data

Multiplication Meltdown: Factors and Multiples / Lisa Arias
(Got Math!)
ISBN 978-1-62717-711-5 (hard cover)
ISBN 978-1-62717-833-4 (soft cover)
ISBN 978-1-62717-946-1 (e-Book)
Library of Congress Control Number: 2014935588

Printed in the United States of America, North Mankato, Minnesota

Also Available as: